HOW *WOULD* YOU SURVIVE AS AN ANCIENT
GREEK?

Written by
Fiona Macdonald

Illustrated by
Mark Bergin

Created & Designed by
David Salariya

W
FRANKLIN WATTS
NEW YORK•LONDON•SYDNEY

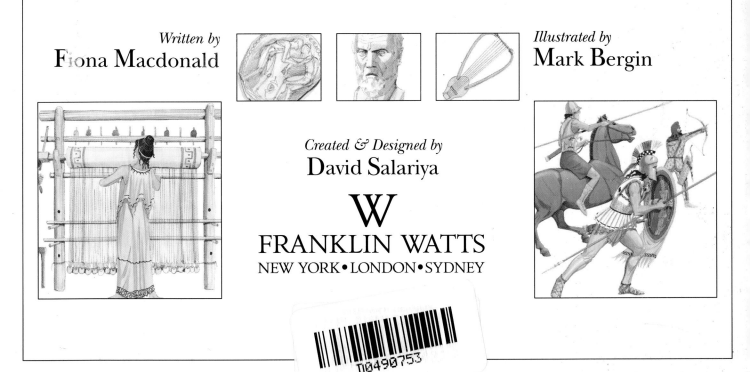

David Salariya — *Director*
Penny Clarke — *Editor*
Henrietta McCall — *Consultant*

FIONA MACDONALD

studied history at Cambridge University and at the University of East Anglia, where she is a part-time Tutor in Medieval History. She has also taught in schools and adult education, and is the author of numerous books for children on historical topics, including **Cities** and **Houses** in the *Timelines* series, **How *Would* You Survive as an Aztec?** and **How *Would* You Survive in the Middle Ages?**

MARK BERGIN

was born in Hastings in 1961. He studied at Eastbourne College of Art and has specialised in historical reconstruction since leaving art school in 1983. He lives in East Sussex with his wife and children.

DAVID SALARIYA

was born in Dundee, Scotland, where he studied illustration and printmaking. He has illustrated a wide range of books on botanical, historical and mythical subjects. He has created and designed many new series of books for publishers in the UK and overseas. In 1989 he established The Salariya Book Company. He lives in Brighton with his wife, the illustrator Shirley Willis.

©THE SALARIYA BOOK CO LTD MCMXCV

Printed in Belgium

A CIP catalogue record for this book is available from the British Library.

First published in 1993
This edition published in 1999

FRANKLIN WATTS
96 Leonard Street
London EC2A 4RH

ISBN 0 7496 3502 9
Dewey Classification Number 938

HENRIETTA McCALL

studied ancient history as part of her egyptology course at Oxford University. She now specialises in Mesopotamia. She has edited several children's books set in antiquity. She is the author of a book on Mesopotamian myths published by the British Museum and is a contributor to the *British Museum's Book of Mythical Beasts*.

CONTENTS

BECOMING AN ANCIENT GREEK

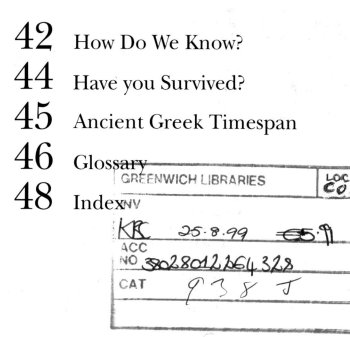

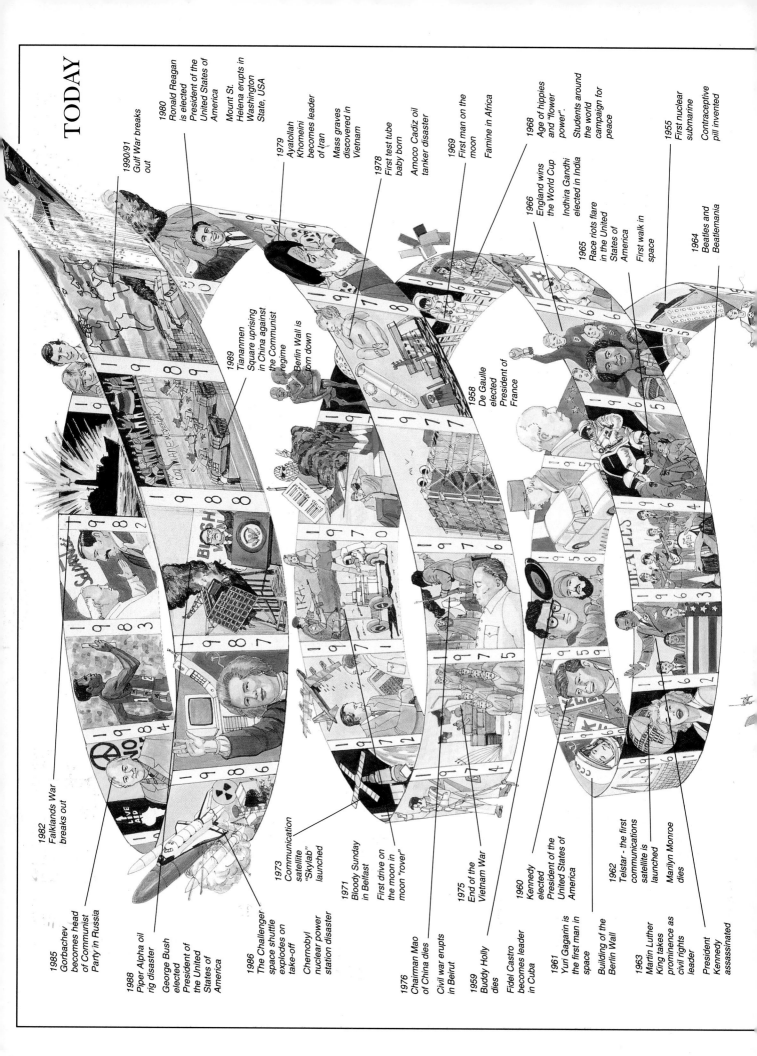

TODAY

1990/91
Gulf War breaks
out

1980
Ronald Reagan
is elected
President of the
United States of
America

Mount St.
Helena erupts in
Washington
State, USA

1979
Ayatollah
Khomeini
becomes leader
of Iran

Mass graves
discovered in
Vietnam

1978
First test tube
baby born

Amoco Cadiz oil
tanker disaster

1969
First man on the
moon

Famine in Africa

1968
Age of hippies
and "flower
power".

Students around
the world
campaign for
peace

1966
England wins
the World Cup

Indhira Gandhi
elected in India

1965
Race riots flare
in the United
States of
America

First walk in
space

1964
Beatles and
Beatlemania

1955
First nuclear
submarine

Contraceptive
pill invented

1989
Tiananmen
Square uprising
in China against
the Communist
regime

Berlin Wall is
torn down

1958
De Gaulle
elected
President of
France

1985
Gorbachev
becomes head
of Communist
Party in Russia

1982
Falklands War
breaks out

1988
Piper Alpha oil
rig disaster

George Bush
elected
President of
the United
States of
America

1986
The Challenger
space shuttle
explodes on
take-off

Chernobyl
nuclear power
station disaster

1973
Communication
satellite
"Skylab"
launched

1971
Bloody Sunday
in Belfast

First drive on
the moon in
moon "rover"

1975
End of the
Vietnam War

1960
Kennedy
elected
President of the
United States of
America

1962
Telstar - the first
communications
satellite is
launched

Marilyn Monroe
dies

1976
Chairman Mao
of China dies

Civil war erupts
in Beirut

1959
Buddy Holly
dies

Fidel Castro
becomes leader
in Cuba

1961
Yuri Gagarin is
the first man in
space

Building of the
Berlin Wall

1963
Martin Luther
King takes
prominence as
civil rights
leader

President
Kennedy
assassinated

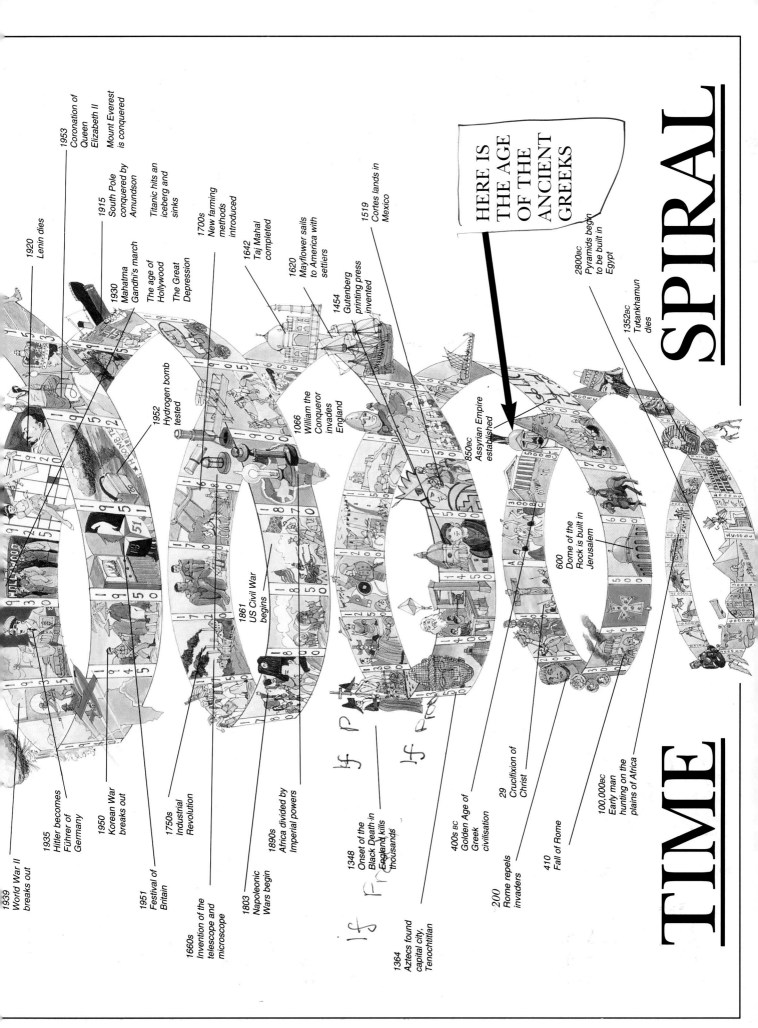

SPIRAL

TIME

HERE IS
THE AGE
OF THE
ANCIENT
GREEKS

1939
World War II
breaks out

1920
Lenin dies

1953
Coronation of
Queen
Elizabeth II

Mount Everest
is conquered

1935
Hitler becomes
Führer of
Germany

1915
South Pole
conquered by
Amundson

Titanic hits an
iceberg and
sinks

1950
Korean War
breaks out

1930
Mahatma
Gandhi's march

The age of
Hollywood

The Great
Depression

1700s
New farming
methods
introduced

1951
Festival of
Britain

1952
Hydrogen bomb
tested

1642
Taj Mahal
completed

1750s
Industrial
Revolution

1620
Mayflower sails
to America with
settlers

1454
Gutenberg
printing press
invented

1519
Cortes lands in
Mexico

1660s
Invention of the
telescope and
microscope

1861
US Civil War
begins

1066
William the
Conqueror
invades
England

2800bc
Pyramids begin
to be built in
Egypt

1803
Napoleonic
Wars begin

1890s
Africa divided by
Imperial powers

850bc
Assyrian Empire
established

1352bc
Tutankhamun
dies

1364
Aztecs found
capital city,
Tenochtitlan

1348
Onset of the
Black Death in
England kills
thousands

400s bc
Golden Age of
Greek
civilisation

600
Dome of the
Rock is built in
Jerusalem

200
Rome repels
invaders

29
Crucifixion of
Christ

410
Fall of Rome

100,000bc
Early man
hunting on the
plains of Africa

Greek Landscape

WHEN YOU ARRIVE in ancient Greece, you will discover a dramatic landscape: high, snow-capped mountains, shady valleys and steep cliffs. There is very little flat land for growing crops; it is mostly a narrow strip along the coast. Many Greeks live in small 'city-states' built there; others live on one of the thousands of rocky islands rising from the brilliant blue sea. The Greeks are very proud of their rugged, beautiful land.

Wildlife

TODAY, there are not many trees on the Greek mountainsides, and the surrounding seas are polluted and dirty in places. But 2,500 years ago, when the ancient Greeks lived, there were thick forests filled with deer, bears and wolves. Swifts and eagles swooped overhead. There were dolphins, porpoises and many fine fish in the sea. In spring, the mountain pastures blazed with wild flowers and were fragrant with herbs.

Gods & Goddesses

AS A TIME-TRAVELLER, you will find out that the ancient Greeks worshipped many gods. Their land was beautiful, but it was also harsh. Summers were very hot, but winters brought icy winds and driving rain. Disease, shipwreck, earthquakes, war (for men) and childbirth (for women) killed people while they were young. That is why Greek men and women said prayers and offered sacrifices to so many gods and goddesses.

Sports & Games

WOULD YOU LIKE to have had the chance to take part in the first Olympic Games? Ancient Greek tradition told that they were first held in 776 BC. Like all Greek festivals, they were held to honour the gods. Over the years, the Games grew into the leading sports festival for the whole of Greece, and winning athletes became famous as heroes. But there were many other local games arranged by different city-states to celebrate their own special gods and festivals.

Education

AS A STUDENT in ancient Greece, you might have the chance to meet some of the most famous scientists, scholars and teachers who ever lived. Their discoveries are still important to modern science. Greeks who could afford it valued learning very highly; boys were sent to study at school, while girls were taught at home. Even ordinary citizens enjoyed plays and stories written by 'world-class' poets. Many people still admire them today.

Family Life

WITH LUCK, you will be invited to visit an ancient Greek family, who pride themselves on their hospitality. What you will see will depend on whether you visit a rich home or a poor one. Ordinary people, in town or country, lived simply; rich farmers and citizens lived in big, well-furnished houses. Often, several generations of a family lived together: grandparents, parents and children. Anyone who could afford to kept slaves.

City-States

SOME GREEKS were farmers, who settled in wild countryside. A few islanders made a living in remote fishing villages. But most Greeks lived in a special type of community known as a 'city-state'. This consisted of a small, self-governing city, plus the surrounding countryside, which it controlled. There were several hundred city-states in ancient Greece. They were all fiercely independent, and often fought among themselves.

Travel & Trade

NOWHERE IN GREECE is very far from the sea, and you will find that the ancient Greeks are skilful sailors. Travel by water is the easiest, though not always the safest, way of getting around. In wintertime, the calm Mediterranean Sea is buffeted by storms, and many pirates lurk, ready to attack. But travel, by sea or along rocky mountain roads, is essential for trade. Greek merchants became rich, importing and exporting goods from many lands.

Women's Lives

WHEN YOU WALKED through the city streets, you may have been surprised to see few women: just female servants and market traders. In the country, you would see only peasant women working in the fields. Where were all the wives of rich citizens and farmers? Mostly, they were at home. This was where they studied, or entertained friends, or worked – it was a responsible job, running a big house or a farm. But they could not take part in public life.

Country Life

YOU WOULD NOTICE that life in the country was very different from life in the towns. There were no busy markets, crowded theatres or sweaty sports centres, and few fine houses or splendid temples. Country people could not hurry out to a nearby stall to buy food; they had to rely on what grew on local farms or on what they could catch when they went hunting in the woods. But they had peace and quiet, fresh air – and less chance of catching diseases.

Arts & Crafts

MUSEUMS TODAY often contain examples of ancient Greek pottery. If you look closely, you will find that it is made of smooth, fine, red clay, painted with dramatic patterns or lively scenes. We know about Greek pottery because a lot of it has survived. But many other skilful Greek craftworkers – jewellers, metalworkers, weavers, sculptors, carpenters – produced goods to the same high standard, as well as simpler everyday items.

Language & Letters

TO THE ancient Greeks, all strangers (including you) were 'barbarians'. They were uncivilised, because they did not speak Greek. For many centuries, the Greek language had not been written down; poems and songs had been memorised and passed on by word of mouth. But, long before the 5th century BC (the time of your visit), Greek scribes had devised an alphabet of letters and sounds from the earlier Phoenician language. It is still used today.

ADRIATIC SEA

MACEDON

Athenian
woman

Athenian
hoplite

Wool

Timber

THRACE

Iron

Copper

← TO ITALY

IONIAN SEA

GREECE

Thebes

Athens

Corinth

Salamis

Lesbos

AEGEAN SEA

Sparta

MEDITERRANEAN SEA

Knossos

CRETE

YOUR MAP OF THE ANCIENT GREEK WORLD

THE WORLD
MAP (above)
shows Greece's
position in
Europe. But the
Greeks were
very well
informed about
distant lands –

from China to
Scandinavia.
Greek
geographers
were probably
the first to
calculate that
the world was
round.

THE PICTURE MAP on these pages shows you the world of
the ancient Greeks: the Mediterranean, the Middle East and
North Africa. You can use it to help you find the places
mentioned in this book, on the Greek mainland and on
islands in the Aegean and Ionian Seas. The map also shows you
Greece's neighbours. Some, like the Persians, were powerful rivals
and, at times, deadly enemies. Others, like the Scythians, sent troops
to help fight alongside Greek soldiers to defend Greek lands. To the
north, the kingdom of Macedon slowly grew
stronger until, by around 350 BC, it was able to
challenge Greek power.

Cyrene

← TO CARTHAGE

AFRICA

LIBYA

Salt

Grain

Ivory

Paper

EGYPT

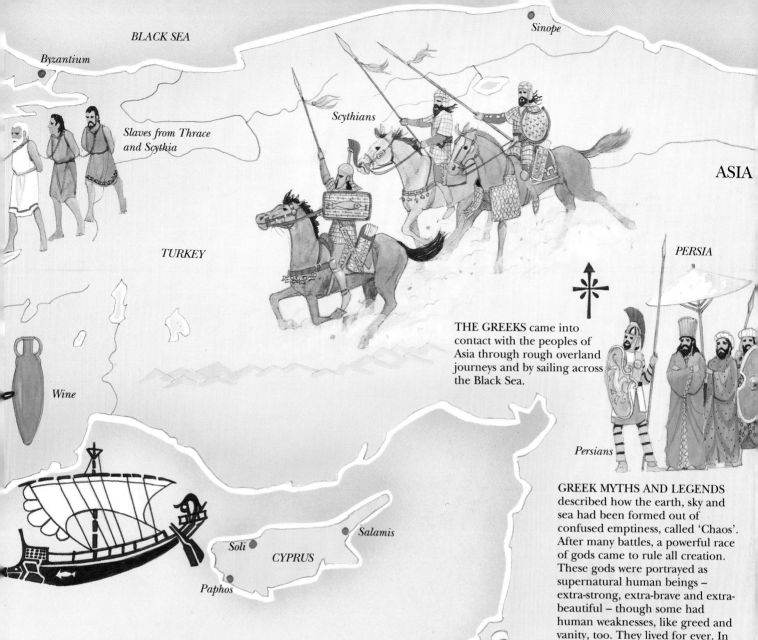

BLACK SEA

Byzantium

Slaves from Thrace and Scythia

Scythians

Sinope

ASIA

TURKEY

PERSIA

THE GREEKS came into contact with the peoples of Asia through rough overland journeys and by sailing across the Black Sea.

Wine

Persians

Soli

Salamis

CYPRUS

Paphos

GREEK MYTHS AND LEGENDS described how the earth, sky and sea had been formed out of confused emptiness, called 'Chaos'. After many battles, a powerful race of gods came to rule all creation. These gods were portrayed as supernatural human beings – extra-strong, extra-brave and extra-beautiful – though some had human weaknesses, like greed and vanity, too. They lived for ever. In order to please the gods, and to ask for their help, the Greeks said prayers, built temples and offered sacrifices. But religious beliefs did not stop some intelligent, Greek people investigating the world around them in a scientific way.

Damascus

Greek colonists settled in little kingdoms that flourished in western Turkey, as well as on the countless islands, and in southern Italy, too. And Greek traders travelled far and wide to strike bargains with merchants in distant lands from Phoenicia in the east to Carthage in the west. Everywhere they went, the Greeks took with them their ideas, beliefs and customs, spreading a rich and brilliant civilisation. Its influence has lasted for thousands of years.

ISRAEL

Jerusalem

Gaza

PHOENICIA

Flax

Slaves

Perfume

WHO OR WHAT are this hunter and his dog afraid of meeting in the forest?
Go to pages 34-35

IS THIS SOLDIER a hoplite? What are his duties? How does he fight?
Go to pages 32-33

WHY IS THIS TREE so important to the economy? Which goddess protects it?
Go to pages 34-35

WHO IS this man? What might he be carrying?
Go to pages 28-29

WHAT DEALS are done in this shady arcade?
Go to pages 24-25

WHAT WILL this man's family have for dinner tonight?
Go to pages 26-27

BEGIN YOUR NEW LIFE HERE

HERE AND ON the next two pages is a panorama of the world
of the ancient Greeks. It is not meant to be a true-to-life
picture, for you would not usually find all these things
happening so close together. It is simply to act as your guide to
this book. Start wherever you wish and follow the Q options.

WHAT is it like
to live in this
city? What
rights do the
citizens have?
Go to pages 30-31

WHY IS this
building such a
strange shape?
Who wears
masks here?
Go to pages 40-41

WHO KEEPS
FIT in this
gymnasium?
Go to pages 18-19

WHAT PRIZES
do top athletes
win?
Go to pages 38-39

WHAT KINDS
of goods could
you buy and sell
here? Where
would they
come from?
Go to pages 24-25

HOW MANY
PEOPLE might
live in a big
town house like
this? What
would they all
do?
Go to pages 16-17

WHERE ARE
this man and
his donkey
going?
Go to pages 24-25

WHAT ARE
these people
making? Will it
taste good?
Go to pages 14-15

WHO IS
worshipped at
these temples?
What happens
outside them?
How were they
built?
Go to pages 34-35

WHAT SORT of
man owns a fast
horse-drawn
chariot like
this?
Go to pages 28-29

WHO ARE
these young
women? Who is
walking with
them?
Go to pages 18-19

WHO WILL
spin and weave
the wool from
sheep and goats
into fine cloth?
Go to pages 22-23

WHAT CROPS is the farmer planning to plant here? What is his plough made of?
Go to pages 14-15

WILL THESE city walls be strong enough to protect you from your enemies?
Go to pages 32-33

WHICH CITY has chosen this owl as its symbol, and portrays it on all its coins?
Go to pages 30-31

WHERE IS this procession going? Who is leading it?
Go to pages 34-35

WHAT INSTRUMENT is this shepherd boy playing? Is it difficult to produce a tune?
Go to pages 40-41

WHAT WILL happen to this ox before long – and why?
Go to pages 34-35

ON THE FARM

WHAT USE COULD YOU MAKE OF THE LAND?

A
S A FARMER, your life was hard. The weather was harsh, the soil was stony and you had to pay a hefty tax to the government. You had few machines to help you – only an ox-drawn plough and simple wooden presses. You knew that only certain crops (chiefly olives, grapes and some grain) would grow on your land, and that only tough mountain sheep and goats would survive and give wool, hides and milk. If you were rich, you would have servants or slaves to help run the farm; your wife and daughters could stay at home while you and your sons supervised everyone else's work. If you were poor, your family would have to manage by itself.

November: Plough the land with a heavy wooden plough, pulled by oxen or mules.

November: After ploughing, sow wheat or barley by hand. Cover the seeds with earth, using a hoe.

December: It is too cold for crops to grow, so use the time to repair farm walls and buildings.

January: Cut down dead branches and gather dead wood to burn on fires to warm the house.

Q

As you live on a farm, the doctors will be pleased with you. Why?
Go to pages 36-37

(Left) You live in a house with thick stone walls and a clay-tiled roof. There are only three rooms: bedroom, living room, and store-room, where food and farm tools are kept. Rafters, doorposts and furniture are made from oak trees you and your slaves have cut down. Windows have strong shutters, to keep robbers out.

February: Plough fallow land to kill the weeds that have started to grow.

March: Prune old, dead twigs from the vines, to encourage new young shoots.

April: The weather is getting warmer. It's time to shear the sheep.

April: The grass has grown well. Cut it and dry it to make the first crop of hay.

May: The barley is beginning to ripen. Make sure your sickles are sharp.

May: Towards the end of May the harvest begins. You cut the ripe barley.

EVERYONE in a farmer's family has to work. You send your sons out every morning to lead the sheep and goats to fresh pasture. It is their job to stop the animals straying or falling over steep cliffs. Sheep and goats are very useful: they provide wool (or hair) for weaving, milk to make cheese, and, when they are old, meat for special feasts.

(Below) You had to be strong to work the olive press. Ripe green olives – still firm and fibrous – were packed into nets then crushed between two heavy stones using a huge, weighted wooden lever. The oil from the olives was used for cooking and to preserve food. Low-grade oil was burned in little lamps, and used to clean and soften the skin.

WILD FOODS

You can go hunting wild boar in the woods, for sport and for food.

In wild mountain country, you might catch wolves, bear or deer.

You can catch fish and shellfish from the sea or from mountain streams.

You can also hunt for birds' nests and steal the eggs to eat.

THE GRAPE-HARVEST

(below) was a busy time for everyone on the farm. Each bunch of grapes was picked by hand, then carried in sticky, oozy baskets to the farmyard, where they were left for 9 days then crushed to extract their juice. This was left to ferment and turn into wine. At first, squashing the grapes was fun, but the sun was hot and crushers soon got tired. Music helped them to keep on 'dancing'.

(Below) If you were a woman in a farming family, you worked hard all year round. In summer, you gathered herbs and 'horta' (wild greens). You grew beans and onions and dried them for winter meals. You kept bees for honey. You milked the sheep and goats, picked apples, gathered nuts and weeded the vegetable garden.

June: The harvest continues. You carry sheaves of wheat to the barns.

June: The harvest continues. You carry sheaves of wheat to the barns.

July: The grapes are getting ripe and sweet. Pick them carefully, for wine.

July: The olives are ready. Get boys to knock the ripe fruit from the trees.

August: Now you winnow the wheat, separating grain from the chaff.

September: Farmers' wives make cheese from goats' milk.

October: Cut down timber for wood to repair buildings; plant new trees.

Q

As a farmer, you'll need the help of the gods. Who do you pray to?
Go to pages 34-35

Go to pages 34-35

IN A TOWN

WHAT WOULD YOUR LIFE BE LIKE?

*Several generations
of your family lived
together. Grand-
parents and parents
were the most
respected.*

*You loved your
children but you
expected them to
be hard-working
and obedient. Boys
and girls were
brought up
differently.*

*If you were rich,
your children would
have tutors and
nursemaids to care
for them and to
teach them.*

*You would have
many household
servants: maids
clean, weave cloth
and look after
young children.*

O RIGINALLY, most Greek people lived and worked in the countryside. But
after around 700 BC, towns, which had existed for centuries as markets
and strongholds, grew bigger and more prosperous through trade and
manufacturing. Poor farmers and their servants migrated there, seeking a
new life and better prospects. Everywhere, the streets seemed full of people, from
proud rich men with bodyguards to beggars in the dirt. The air was noisy with
hammering, shouting and the clatter of horses' hooves. It was also very smelly; there
were no sewers. At night, servants with torches escorted groups of partygoers and
kept a lookout for thieves.

*As a craftworker in a town, you
live in a house like this. It is
one in a block of homes for
10 families. Your house
is built round a
courtyard, containing
the family altar where
you make offerings to
the gods. It is
shielded from the
street by a strong
gate and high wall.*

Family bedrooms

Family living rooms

Women's room

*Shop and
storeroom*

*Your house is well-
designed, with
rooms for preparing
and cooking food,
entertaining guests,
and storing and
selling craft goods
you have made.
There are also
private family living
rooms, bedrooms
and workrooms for
female members of
the family and their
women slaves.*

*Porch and
entrance*

Kitchen

Store room

Work room

*You work at home,
in a studio at the
front of your house.
Customers can
walk in from the
street to admire
your work in
progess.*

Q

Noisy, dirty town
life is making
you feel ill.
Where can you
find a doctor?
Go to pages 36-37

*Maids also help rich
women to dress
and to arrange their
hair.*

*Your male servants
do heavy house-
work, guard the door,
and run errands.*

*Your cooks and
their helpers work
hard in the kitchen,
preparing meals.*

*Your food is served
by young boys,
chosen for their
good manners.*

*You own a country
estate; the farm
manager is a wise,
trusted servant.*

*If you are a crafts-
man, your servants
work as assistants,
making fine goods.*

Upper open balcony

IF YOU WERE VERY RICH, perhaps one of the leaders of the government, you would live in a fine town house like this, with a grand entrance portico, decorated with carved marble columns.

Family bedrooms

GREEK FURNITURE

If you were rich, your house would be furnished with comfortable couches, to lie on at mealtimes.

Your mother might sit on an elegant chair like this, with her feet resting on a footstool.

Living room

Food store

WE KNOW ABOUT LIFE in ancient Greek towns as a result of excavations by archaeologists at sites such as Priene (below). There, they have uncovered a complete, planned town, with well-laid out streets, a secure acropolis (central fortress), temples, markets, a gymnasium, sports arena, government meeting-house and a theatre.

You would stand tables beside the couches in the dining room. They had three legs, which balanced better than four.

YOUR HOUSE would be designed to impress visitors with your wealth and artistic good taste, as well as to provide a comfortable home for your family.

Open courtyard 'peristyle'

Lavatory

You would invite visitors to sit on stools with padded seats. Your servants sat on rough wooden seats or on the floor.

Towns were also home to slaves and other non-citizens: travelling merchants, craftsmen, scholars and sailors. Overcrowding – and disputes about town government – sometimes led to problems. Athens (population 250,000) faced famine, plague, bitter political rivalry and slave revolts. Even so, for many Greeks, town life was best.

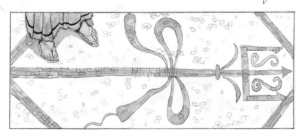

What sort of floor would you like? You can have stone slabs, baked clay *tiles, or a pebble mosaic. You ask the master craftsman to design* *a pattern just for you. This mosaic floor shows the god Poseidon's trident.*

How to make a pebble mosaic: go to the seashore and collect lots of

coloured pebbles, all the same size. Sort them carefully. Then prepare a

'bed' of soil or sand. Hammer your pebbles into this, to make a pattern.

Q

You have an idea about improving the way your town is run. What will you do about it?
Go to pages 24-25

YOUR FAMILY
WHO WOULD LIVE WITH YOU?

As a wife, your most important task was to give birth to children, to continue your husband's family.

A S AN ANCIENT GREEK, your family was very important. It gave you food and shelter, education, training for work or a career in politics, and would probably find you a marriage partner. Your 'family' often included slaves and servants living in your home. Like everyone else, they were your father's responsibility. He could send you away to be adopted and even divorce your mother or marry her to someone else against her will.

A Greek woman was valued for what she did for others (being faithful to her husband and creating a comfortable home), not for what she did to fulfil herself. In the warlike city of Sparta, women's lives were different. They were well-educated, independent, took part in politics, and even joined in sports, wearing so little that other Greeks were shocked. A Spartan woman was expected to be as brave as a man; mothers encouraged their sons to die in battle, rather than face defeat.

You were also responsible for running the household and managing the servants.

As a family, you worshipped together, but you were not all equal. Men were in charge. They protected and provided for women and children, but they also controlled them. In most Greek states (except Sparta) women could not own property, and had always to be under the legal guardianship of a man – husband, father or other male relative.

You knew how to weave fine fabrics for clothing, and how to make rugs and tapestries to decorate your home.

If you were poor, you would also have to do all the cooking and housework as well.

A GREEK WEDDING

Greek children were toilet trained by using clever clay potty-seats like this.

Q

Your daughter wants to take part in the Olympic Games. What do you say to her?
Go to pages 38-39

Boys and girls from poor families might meet and fall in love as they worked on the farm.

Rich, noble girls were not allowed to go out alone. Their marriages were arranged for them.

Before the wedding, the bride made an offering to Artemis, goddess of all women.

The bride's parents gave a dowry of land, money or fine goods to the bridegroom's family.

On the wedding day, the bride left for the bridegroom's house – her new home.

The day after the wedding, friends came to visit, bringing presents with them.

As a schoolboy, you would learn to read and write, how to calculate using an abacus, how to sing and recite poetry – pupils had to memorise the words by heart – and how to do 'gymnastics', which included running, jumping, wrestling and throwing the javelin. Greek teachers aimed at producing a well-balanced individual, with 'a healthy mind in a healthy body'.

CHILDREN'S TOYS

Clay model of a man riding on the back of a goose. Children's toys were often buried with them in tombs. Can you think why?

Another toy animal. Rabbits were native to Mediterranean lands; like small birds, they were sometimes kept as children's pets.

Boys might be beaten if their teachers felt they were not trying hard enough to win.

A baby's rattle, shaped like a pig. It is made of baked and painted clay, with noisy clay beads inside.

Training races were run on sand, to encourage strength and endurance. Sport was such an important part of education that the ancient Greek word 'gymnasium', which meant 'boys' school', has now come to mean 'sports hall'.

If you were a rich girl, you would not be allowed to leave home or go to school. Your education would include traditional female skills, like spinning and weaving, as well as learning to read, write and calculate. Your mother would teach you ancient, secret songs and dances so that you could take part in special women's festivals held in honour of Athena and other great goddesses.

This clay doll was treasured by a child who lived 2500 years ago. The legs and arms were fixed with leather thongs, so they could move.

THE ALPHABET

A B Γ Δ E Z H Θ I K Λ M N Ξ O Π P Σ T Y Φ X Ψ Ω

α β γ δ ε ζ η θ ι κ λ μ ν ξ ο π ρ σ τ υ φ χ ψ ω

A B C D E Z E Th I K L M N X O P R S T U Ph Kh Ch Ps O

The Greeks invented a way of writing using symbols for different sounds.

Above, you can see these Greek symbols, capital letters and small letters.

We still use these Greek letters, as 'modernised' by the Romans about 2000 years ago.

The word alphabet comes from the names of the first two: alpha and beta.

But there are some differences between the Greek and modern alphabets. Can you spot them?

Paper was scarce and expensive, so Greeks wrote on wooden tablets coated with wax.

Q

You plan to take your family to the theatre. Will your slaves come too?
Go to pages 40-41

YOUR CLOTHES
WHAT WOULD YOU WEAR?

IF YOU WERE A GREEK MAN, you might spend quite a large part of your time wearing very few clothes, or even none at all. For sports, swimming, working in hot weather or in hot places – down the mines or in a potter's kiln-room – nakedness seemed practical and sensible. But when women were around men wore clothes. As a woman, unless you were a prostitute or a dancing girl, you were expected to be 'decently' covered. In public, rich or noble women covered their heads and lower faces with a veil.

Greek men also admired naked bodies from an artistic point of view, rather as they might admire a prize horse, or a splendid sunset.

Greek clothes were very simple – little sewing was required. Different styles could easily be created with clever folding and a few pins. Quality was shown by beautifully spun fabrics and dyed or embroidered trims.

Hollow gold bracelet decorated with lions' heads. Threaded through it, a necklace of silver beads ornamented with face-shaped silver plaques.

HATS & HAIRSTYLES

Summer temperatures reached 30°C, so peasants wore few clothes for work.

In the winter, it was cooler. Peasants wore caps and tunics of rough homespun wool, and leather boots.

For journeys, it was sensible to take a warm cloak and a waterproof leather hat to protect you from wind and rain.

As a Greek, you like keeping clean. If you are rich and live near a stream you might have the water diverted to flow through your home. But you are more likely to take baths in a big clay tub, filled with water from the well.

Upper-class women were careful to shade their delicate complexions from the hot Greek sun.

Sunshade

Mirror

DORIC CHITON, or tunic. Sometimes the linen fabric was pleated by twisting it tightly when wet. You could add a belt round your waist if you liked.

WEALTHY GREEK WOMEN employed specially-trained servants to arrange their hair and make-up. They kept their cosmetics (coloured earths and berry juices) in beautiful silver boxes and jars.

Q

Where does the silver used to make the bracelets you are wearing come from?
Go to pages 32-33

Greek men adopted many hairstyles. Spartan warriors were famous for their long curls.

Cavalrymen wore hat-shaped helmets made of bronze and covered with woollen cloth.

Other soldiers wore simple 'pot-shaped' caps like this. It was made of leather and metal.

Army commanders from Sparta wore splendid full-face helmets with feather crests.

For working in the fields, peasants might wear shady hats of plaited straw.

Greeks admired beards as 'manly'. Men combed, oiled and trimmed their beards with care.

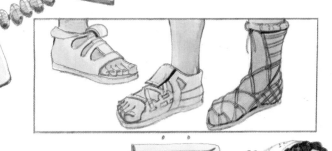

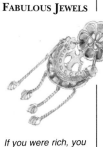

Whether you were a man or a woman, you usually went barefoot. On very rough ground, men wore sandals like these. They were made of leather, treated with oak-bark and polished with olive oil to make them last. Sometimes they had cork soles, for extra comfort. Women's sandals were simpler – just soles and thongs. Popular colours were red and yellow.

High fashion in Athens around 450 BC. For a woman, a 'peplos' of fine wool, edged with an expensive purple dyed border, worn over a long chiton of cool white linen. For a man, a short chiton, also of linen, covered by an elegantly-draped wool 'himation'

If you were rich, you would wear beautiful gold earrings like these, which jingled as you walked.

You would show off your pale-skinned arms (only peasants and servants got suntanned) by wearing bracelets.

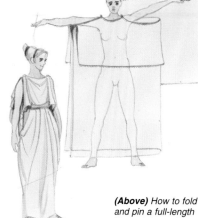

(Above) How to fold and pin a full-length Doric-style woollen tunic, called a 'peplos'. It was traditionally worn by women.

You would order your maid to arrange gold and silver pins decorated with jewelled flowers in your hair.

(Below) After around 500 BC, a new style of long linen tunic, called an Ionian chiton, became popular. It originated in Turkey.

Round your neck, you would wear fine ropes woven from gold and silver wire, with engraved gemstone pendants.

All Greek women let their hair grow long; it was shameful to cut it.

WOMEN'S HAIR

Hair could be coiled in a knot and then held in place by a metal band or 'diadem'.

Long thick hair could be plaited, then loosened to display glossy, bouncy curls.

It was essential to have a maid if you wanted a style based on elaborate braids.

Women from northern Greece sometimes hid their hair under woollen caps.

It was acceptable for young, unmarried girls to let their hair flow over their shoulders.

Older women often covered their hair with a scarf. They sometimes added a veil too.

Q

Why should your doctor be well-dressed?
Go to pages 36-37

IN THE WORKSHOPS

HOW WOULD YOU MAKE A LIVING?

POTTERY

Athenian craft-workers made many kinds of pottery. **(Above)** Krater, for mixing wine and water at meals.

(Above) Hydria, for carrying water from the kitchen to the dining room.
(Below) Stamnos, or storage jar.

The shape of each pot depended on how it was to be used.
(Below) Psycter, or wine-cooler.

Psycter pots were sprinkled with water. As it evaporated, the wine inside cooled. This shape gave maximum surface area for cooling.

TRADITIONALLY, the Greeks admired craftwork. At one time, every Athenian father was meant to make sure his son learned a trade. But that was long ago. By the 5th century BC, towns in Greece were full of specialist craft-workers of all kinds, from carpenters and shoemakers to potters, armourers and goldsmiths. Some of these workers produced solid everyday goods for ordinary families to buy. Others were top-class artists, producing splendid masterpieces for rich, powerful patrons, and occasionally, like Phidias, a well-known sculptor, becoming their friends.

One of your tasks, as a well-off woman or a humble servant girl, would be to weave cloth using an upright loom. Warp threads were kept taut by stones or clay weights. Different-coloured weft threads were woven in between them, producing beautiful patterns. Before starting to weave, you would also have to clean and comb the wool, spin it into thread, and dye it, too.

Woman using a rare lap spindle. Wool was rolled on it and the thread drawn out.

Lap spindle

Q

What a relief – you won't have to work tomorrow. Why is that?
Go to pages 34-35

Oinochoe, or wine jug. The curled lip made it easy to pour without drips.

Amphora, used for storing liquids. It has strong handles for carrying.

Kylix, or wide drinking cup, designed for two people.

Kantharos, or small cup used for drinking milk or wine.

Alabastron, used to store small amounts of precious oils and perfumes.

Lekythos, for pouring olive oil when cooking or at the dining table.

IF YOU HAD BEEN TRAINED as a potter, you would throw pots on a foot-powered wheel, leave them to get leather-hard, paint them with black or white paint, then fire them in a dome-shaped kiln, heated red-hot by burning wood. Scenes of myths and legends about the gods were popular decorations.

Sculptors carved statues and tombstones from glittering white marble.

Leatherworkers made boots, sandals and workers' aprons from ox and goat hides.

Carpenters made wooden doors and window-shutters, and furniture, too.

ATHENIAN POTTERS used two different painting techniques. Black-figure pottery was produced first; around 600-450 BC. Figures were drawn in black paint, leaving a plain red clay background.

Leading craftsmen and artists were in demand all over Greece. Cities and noble families competed with one other to see who could hire the best. Among ordinary families, women still practised the traditional craft skills of spinning and weaving flax and wool at home.

RED FIGURE pottery was produced later, around 450-350 BC. To make it, potters covered most of the pot's surface with paint, leaving just the scenes they wanted to portray as plain red clay.

TO MAKE IRON you need a kiln like this. It is made of bricks lined with clay, and filled with layers of charcoal and iron ore. As the charcoal burns, the iron melts and trickles down to form a lump, or 'bloom' on the kiln floor. This can be re-melted and hammered into shape.

Weavers used bright-coloured wool to make patterned cloaks, blankets and rugs.

Like other artists, potters signed their best work with their names.

Silver, used for coins and jewellery, came from mines. The best mines

were at Laurium, near Athens. They were worked by slaves. Conditions

were terrible. Criminals were sent there as punishment. Many died.

Silver coin from Athens, decorated with an owl, symbol of goddess Athena.

Silver might be melted with gold to make 'electrum', used for jewellery.

Q

You've had a busy day and now you're hungry. What will you have for dinner?
Go to pages 26-27

GOING TO MARKET

WHAT WOULD YOU BUY AND SELL?

Ceramic vase

THE FIRST GREEK MARKETS were places where farmers met to barter, or exchange, produce, with many arguments about who was getting the best deal. Trade became easier after around 690 BC, when coins were invented in Lydia (in present-day Turkey). By 590 BC, they were widely used in Greece. Powerful cities, like Athens, tried to make everyone use their coins (this helped their own traders), and built large, central market-places, surrounded by buildings where bankers, money-changers, scribes and market officials could set up their stalls. In many big towns and cities, there were separate markets for different goods. But a Greek market-place was more than just somewhere to go shopping, or to sell the goods you had made, or see your neighbours and friends. In many places it was where men gathered to discuss politics and argue about the best way to run their town.

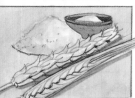

Wheat to make bread was imported from lands north of the Black Sea.

Timber to build ships came from Turkey and the Balkans.

Salted fish was sent from the Greek islands to cities on the mainland.

Dyestuffs and luxury fabrics came from Phoenicia and from Carthage.

VISITING the market-place in a busy Greek city was always entertaining. You could admire the goods on sale, find a real bargain, or just watch the people.

Q

You're tired of gossiping. With a friend, you go to visit a craftsman. Do you need to make an appointment?
Go to pages 16-17

Papyrus – a type of rough paper made from reeds – came from Egypt.

Slave-traders raided lands all round the Mediterranean for captives to sell.

Usually, Greek cities paid for imported goods with silver coins.

Sometimes they exchanged goods: top-quality wine was in demand.

Greek pottery was admired in many lands, and sold for high prices.

Greek olive oil was exported throughout the lands around the Mediterranean.

BLACK SEA

ASIA MINOR

Corinth • • Athens
• Syracuse Sparta
Carthage • • Miletos

MEDITERRANEAN SEA

PHOENICIA

• Cyrene

Greek colonies

The great agora (market-place) in Athens.

Merchants from Greek cities travelled widely in search of goods to bring home to Greece to sell.

Other Greeks decided to seek their fortunes by emigrating to neighbouring lands. Colonists still

thought of themselves as Greek, and maintained close ties with their old cities.

The Greeks used an abacus as a way of calculating quickly. The beads on each row were moved from left to right.

9
90
900

1
10
100

Beads on the top row show numbers 1 to 10; the middle row shows numbers 10 to 100; the bottom row shows numbers 100 to 1,000.

This example shows the number 235. How would you move the beads to add 123 and make a new total of 358?

Lightweight coins and heavy goods could all be weighed on balance scales.

GREEK COINS

Silver coin made in Athens around 450 BC. It shows Athena's head.

Silver coin showing an ancient hero made in Macedon around 330 BC.

Silver coin from Syracuse in Sicily showing Arethusa, a water-nymph.

Reverse of the coin from Syracuse, showing a chariot race.

Silver coin from Corinth, showing Pegasus, a magical winged horse.

Silver coin from the island of Aegina, showing a turtle from the sea.

Q

How do the merchants and farmers bring their goods to market?
Go to pages 28-29

YOUR FOOD
WHAT WOULD YOU EAT AND DRINK?

H OW WOULD YOU SURVIVE on an ancient Greek diet? Your food would be simple – bread, milk, beans, olives, grapes, figs, and, in summer, fresh vegetables and herbs. In winter, you would eat apples, chestnuts, lentils and smelly goats' cheese. You didn't have sugar, but you might buy delicious honey from mountain farms. If you lived by the coast, you would eat fish and sea creatures – urchins, octopus and squid. Food like this was very healthy, if you could get enough of it. As the population grew, famine was always a possibility. And in wartime, armies set fire to crops in the fields, trying to starve their enemies into surrender. Cooking was normally done by Greek wives and daughters, although in many families husbands did the shopping. Wealthy people had slaves to work in their kitchens, and specially-trained cooks to prepare dinner party meals.

Terracotta model of a butcher with his chopper, killing a piglet, made around 450 BC.

Crush grain in a big stone bowl using a heavy grinding stone. This is women's work.

Add water, olive oil and a little cloudy wine; this contains yeast which will help the bread rise. Mix well.

Turn the bread onto a table and knead well. Shape into a round flat loaf and leave to rise.

Bake your bread in a clay oven, which you have heated in advance with wood.

(Below) Only the rich could afford to eat these foods every day.

If you were a rich man, one of your favourite ways of spending an evening would be relaxing with your friends at a 'symposium', or dinner party. You washed, changed into clean clothes, put on some scent and arrived on time; it was rude to be late. You left your dusty shoes at the door, and washed your hands and feet. In the dining room, you were offered a couch to sit or lie on, then slaves carried in a table, arranged with food and wine.

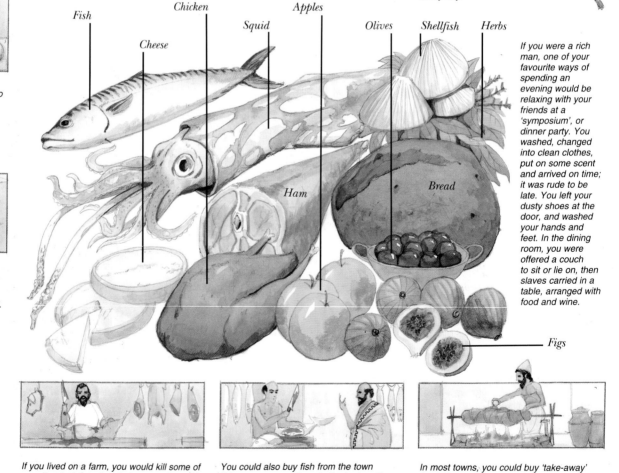

Fish · Cheese · Chicken · Squid · Apples · Ham · Olives · Shellfish · Herbs · Bread · Figs

Q

Your mistress tells you to bring olive oil to the dining table. What do you use to carry it?
Go to pages 22-23

If you lived on a farm, you would kill some of your livestock for meat. In towns, you would buy meat from a butcher's shop or a market stall.

You could also buy fish from the town fishmonger, or go down to the harbour to buy fresh fish from the fishermen as they landed their catch.

In most towns, you could buy 'take-away' foods from cooked meat shops and stalls. Busy cooks roasted meat on spits over charcoal fires.

All water for
drinking had to be
carried, usually by
women, from wells
or from mountain
springs.

Wine was carried in
sewn-up goatskins,
which were
transported by
donkey or mule.

Wine was nearly
always drunk
diluted with water;
they were mixed
together in big
bowls then ladled
into cups.

Drinking cups could
be very elaborate.
This cup, made for
a very rich family, is
shaped like a
magical beast.

*Wine cup
shaped like a
ram's head.*

As a guest, you
hoped your meal
would be delicious,
but you also looked
forward to the main
point of the evening:
good companionship
and lively
discussions on
topics of all kinds.

Sometimes, guests
at dinner-parties
drank too much, as
this Athenian vase-
painting shows.
They might also
prefer listening to
music, or watching
naked slave girls (or
boys) dancing,
instead of making
intelligent
conversation.

HOW TO PLAY KOTTABOS

Kottabos was a favourite game played at
dinner-parties for men. First, drink lots of
wine. Drunkenness was allowed at parties
like these.

Leave a little wine in the bottom of a drinking
cup. A wide cup makes the game more
difficult; it is more awkward to handle than a
narrow one.

Fix a target on a wall or put a pot on a
stand. Fling your wine at it, calling out your
lover's name. The person whose wine lands
nearest the target is the most faithful lover.

Q

What has your
doctor told you
about healthy
foods and a
healthy
lifestyle?
Go to pages 36-37

You are a sailor. What is your ship like? It might be a big merchant ship, with a wide hull to hold lots of cargo.

Or it might be a small fishing boat, which you row out into the bay every evening when the sun goes down.

Perhaps it is a man-of-war, with a jutting ram at the prow, with which to hole enemy ships underwater.

Your man-of-war is powered by tiers of oarsmen sitting below decks, as well as by wind trapped in a big square sail.

Q

Who would help you measure the distance you had travelled on a long journey?
Go to pages 36-37

THE EARLIEST Greek ships were fairly small (maybe 30 metres long) with one bank of oars and a simple sail, like this galley from the 6th century BC shown on an Athenian vase.

LONG JOURNEYS
WHERE WOULD YOU TRAVEL?

AS A GREEK CITIZEN, you would be patriotic. You spoke a Greek dialect, followed Greek customs and worshipped Greek gods. Your homeland was best, but you knew there was a wider world beyond your own frontiers. The best way to travel there – for trade, exploration, or to found a new colony – was usually by sea, sailing from island to island or along the coast. Greek sailors did not like to venture far out of sight of land. They had no compasses to help them steer or fix their position and relied on the stars. Winter storms made the seas dangerous; many ships were wrecked.

LATER, magnificent warships like this trireme crewed by 200 men were built. In the 5th century BC, at the height of its power, Athens had 300.

Shipbuilding tools:
a. Curved saw.
b. Straight saw.
c. Axe.
d. Mallet.
e. Adze.
f. Chisel.

Greek boats were made of planks of wood, nailed to a wooden frame.

A huge eye was painted on the side of the hull, to keep away the 'evil eye'.

You might meet travellers like this on bumpy Greek roads: **a.** army porter, carrying food, tools and equipment. **b.** rich man's groom, driving his master's two-horse cart. **c.** young traveller, riding a fast, well-bred horse. **d.** army officer and driver, in a four-horse war chariot.

The Greek landscape made overland travel difficult, but there were some roads. Narrow mountain passes were for walkers or sure-footed mules. Better paths ran along the coast in eastern Greece where the mountains sloped gently down to the sea. They were built for wheeled traffic: fast chariots or lumbering farm carts stacked with huge clay jars of grain.

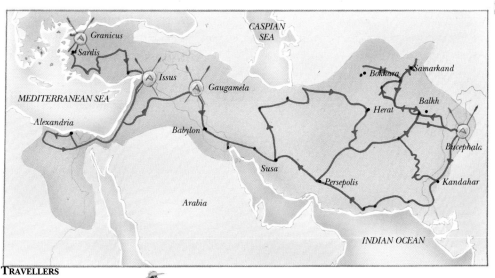

TRAVELLERS

Merchants and farm servants travelled from the countryside to the towns, leading donkeys and mules carrying panniers full of goods to sell in the market.

Government messengers, bold explorers and mysterious army spies travelled on foot, running swiftly along steep, rocky mountain paths.

The first-ever marathon (490 BC) was an heroic run by an Athenian soldier, from Marathon to Athens (40 km), to bring news of victory in battle against Persia.

ALEXANDER THE GREAT

One of the most famous travellers of the time was Alexander the Great, (356-323 BC) warrior king of Macedon, a country north of Greece. In 334 BC, he set out with his army to conquer the vast empire of the Persians, traditional enemies of Macedon and the Greeks. He achieved this after winning the battle of Gaugamela in 331 BC.

ALEXANDER'S search for new lands to conquer led him and his troops across wild, mountainous Central Asia to the borders of India. He died at Babylon on his way home.

NEW COLONIES

You are a Greek islander. Your homeland is over-crowded and poor. Each winter, you go hungry. What can you do?

You decide to emigrate with your family to a new colony in Turkey or southern Italy.

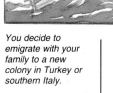

But life there is harsh. You have to clear the soil and build a house. The local people are hostile; you miss Greek life.

So you set off back 'home'. But a new man is now village chief. He knows the island cannot feed any more people. He will not let you land.

Q

Where could you set out for and be sure of a safe journey?
Go to pages 38-39

Women in Athens and elsewhere were not allowed to vote or take part in government.

Foreigners had no rights to vote, even if they had been living in Greece for many years.

Slaves were never treated equally with free citizens, so they could not vote or be chosen for government office.

As a punishment for bad behaviour, criminals lost many civil rights, including the right to vote.

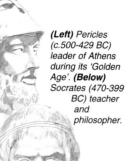

(Left) Pericles (c.500-429 BC) leader of Athens during its 'Golden Age'. **(Below)** Socrates (470-399 BC) teacher and philosopher.

SOCRATES was a famous philosopher and an inspiring teacher, who encouraged his students to question and challenge existing ideas. But he lived at a time of political unrest, and the government accused him of 'corrupting the young', that is, of teaching them to criticise society and the government. He was condemned to death. In fact, Socrates had not wanted to break the law. He simply hoped to teach his students how to tell good government from bad. To show his respect for the rule of law, he agreed to commit suicide by drinking poison in 399 BC.

As an adult male citizen of an ancient Greek city-state, you had the right to take part in government by voting at meetings which discussed and decided policies and plans.

POLITICS AND LAWS

HOW WOULD YOU HELP RUN THE GOVERNMENT?

DEMOCRACY WAS BORN in the city-state of Athens during the period 500-400 BC. 'Demokratia' is a Greek word, meaning 'rule by the people'. But how did it work?

Greece was divided into several hundred city-states, each made up of a town or city and the farmland all around. Some city-states were small, with just a few thousand citizens. Athens was the largest and strongest, and had a rich overseas empire.

ATHENIAN SILVER COIN, made 480-460 BC. It shows the goddess Athena's owl and an olive branch, both symbols of Athens' imperial power.

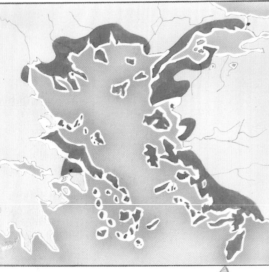

THE ATHENIAN EMPIRE c.450 BC. All the cities of the empire paid a regular tribute, usually of silver, to the government in Athens.

This carved stone tribute list for 440-439 BC records that one-sixtieth (between 1 and 2 per cent) of the tribute received by the Athenian government was given to the temple of Athena.

Q

How could you criticise politicians you disagreed with without making a speech?
Go to pages 40-41

Go to pages 40-41

Speeches at the public assembly ('ecclesia') were timed by a water-clock. The top jar was filled with water which ran slowly into the lower jar. When the top jar was empty, it was time to end your speech.

Government leaders (including generals in the army) were chosen by Athenian citizens voting at public elections. Citizens also voted in criminal trials. They put clay ballots (one shape for innocent, another for guilty into

a bin. Verdicts were based on majority votes. Citizens punished bad politicians by voting to banish ('ostracise') them for 10 years. They scratched the names on bits of pot, which were collected and counted.

The assembly in Athens met every nine days. About 5000 citizens found time to attend. Meetings were often noisy and argumentative.

ATHENIAN IDEAS

As an Athenian citizen, you would think of your city as the most civilised place in the world.

You would be very proud of its democratic style of government, based on votes at the assembly.

You would believe that it was better to solve conflicts through intelligent discussion than by fighting.

But if your city or its possessions were attacked, you would be willing to fight and die to defend them.

The earliest city-states were ruled by warlords or (in Sparta) kings. In the 6th century BC, many 'tyrants', strong men discontented with old-style government, seized power. Other states were ruled by 'oligarchs', un-elected, wealthy men. But in the 5th century BC, a new form of 'democratic' government developed. All important decisions were made at public assemblies. Any adult male citizen could attend, make speeches and vote. Assemblies used lotteries to choose officials, juries for the courts and army commanders. For urgent decisions and routine administration, there was a council of 500 men, also chosen by lot. No-one could be a councillor for more than two years, spreading power among ordinary people.

Athena

To give thanks to Athena, and to show his city's power, Pericles commissioned a magnificent temple, the Parthenon, to house this huge (11 metre) statue, dedicated in 438 BC.

SPARTAN SKILLS

Boys were taken away from their parents at 7 years old, to go to warrior training school.

At school, they learned survival skills: to be tough, brave and obedient. Discipline was harsh.

Teachers said boys must always hide their feelings: 'Smile, even if your brother is killed.'

Boys also learned to be cunning; they were taught to steal, even taking holy food from temples.

They were taught to jeer at the weak. This was to scare them into always doing their best.

Warriors slept in cold rooms and were fed plain 'black broth' to keep them fit and tough.

Q

As a wealthy citizen, how could you impress your friends?
Go to pages 22-23

He fought with bow and arrows, weapons the Greeks did not normally use.

Wealthy cities like Athens paid peoples from other lands to join their army. This Scythian soldier came from the shores of the Black Sea.

Bottom map: 490 BC, by sea. The Persians were defeated at the battle of Marathon. 480 BC, overland. The Persians won at Thermopylae and sacked Athens, but were then defeated at Salamis and Plataea and had to retreat.

Top map: The Persian empire around 500 BC.

AS A CITIZEN, it was your duty to fight to defend your homeland. You had to be prepared to leave your home and family when the government called you to fight. If you were rich, you supplied your own horse, weapons and armour, otherwise, you borrowed them from army stores.

Routes of the two greatest Persian invasions of Greece.

Thermopylae

Salamis

Persian army in 480 BC

Persian fleet in 490 BC

Q

You want your father to come back safe from the war. Who should you sacrifice to?
Go to pages 34-35

Athenian cavalry officer with chariot-driver in a fast horse-drawn chariot.

In battle, officers climbed on chariots to shout orders and get a better view of the fighting.

Athenian hoplite, a foot soldier. He wears leather body armour, bronze helmet and greaves.

Ephebe (young, trainee soldier). Each spear is 2 or 3 metres long and tipped with bronze.

In hand-to-hand fighting, a hoplite relied on his sharp iron sword and his 'hoplon' (shield).

Peltasts threw spears or stones. Stones from a sling could pierce flesh at 100 metres.

Many Greek sports, such as wrestling, were excellent training for war. They built up strength and fitness.

AT WAR

WHO WERE YOUR ENEMIES?

Persian soldiers fought with bows and arrows, short spears and sharp daggers. They carried large shields of woven twigs.

Persian soldiers belonged to an 'immortal' army, an army that never died. It was given this name because it was kept at a

constant strength of 10,000 men. As soon as one soldier was killed, a reserve was brought in to fill his place.

As part of their training, soldiers went running in full armour. One day, they might need to run for their lives on the battlefield.

GREEK CITY-STATES WERE RIVALS, and were often at war. There were defensive wars, too, against foreign enemies, especially Persia. Within city-states, civil unrest broke out between rich and poor, opposing political parties, or masters and slaves. A well-trained army was therefore essential, although few city-states were as dedicated to warfare as Sparta. All its male citizens were soldiers, and the city was run like an army camp. Originally, Greek battle commanders relied on elite cavalry troops, recruited from noble families. But gradually, by around 700 BC, battles came to be won by ordinary citizens, fighting shoulder to shoulder as hoplites (foot-soldiers), or rowing in navy ships.

For young, wealthy noblemen, who hoped to become army officers, it was important to learn to ride a horse.

What would you do if you found hills full of silver, right on your doorstep? In 482 BC, silver-rich ores were discovered at Laurium, close to Athens. The Athenians decided to spend this windfall on building a powerful new fleet, to fight off a threatened Persian invasion. Their decision proved to be a wise one. In 480 BC, Persian warships were decisively defeated at a great sea battle at Salamis.

Throwing the javelin was a popular sport; it was also an essential skill for soldiers to learn.

Hoplite wearing a helmet with a stripy horsehair crest. Armour was passed from father to son.

After a victory, Greek troops hung weapons in trees, as offerings to the gods.

Athena's statue in the Parthenon was surrounded by weapons of the Greeks' enemies.

*Painted wooden shields. **(Left)** A scorpion, the badge of a particular troop or town. **(Right)** A gorgon's head. Legends told how the gorgon's gaze turned enemies to stone. A shield like this weighed over 8 kilos.*

Token from an army store, hung on a soldier's name-peg to show he was using state armour.

Q

What would you fear if you heard there was war in Egypt?
Go to pages 24-25

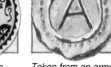

GODS & GODDESSES

If you were an ancient Greek, which god or goddess would you pray to? Zeus was king of the gods. He was all-powerful.

Hera was the wife of Zeus. She was queen of the heavens. She protected married women and their children.

Athena was the daughter of Zeus. She was stern and wise. She protected the city of Athens, and olive trees.

Apollo was the god of music. He was bold, brave and very handsome. He protected singers and poets.

Q

You want a lyre like the musicians in the procession. Your father won't buy you one. What do you do?

Go to pages 40-41

THE ACROPOLIS AT ATHENS

a. Grand entrance and gateway.
b. Temple of Nike (goddess of victory).
c. Brauroneion (temple of Artemis).
d. Chalkotheke (store for holy objects used in temples).
e. Parthenon (temple of Athena).
f. Shrine of Pandion (an ancient hero).

g. Shrine of Zeus.
h. Altar of Athena.
i. Erechtheion (temple of Poseidon and Athena).
j. Arrephorion (house for young girls serving the goddess

Athena).
k. Statue of Athena (could be seen by sailors out at sea – used as a welcoming beacon).

You are excited because it is a festival day. There will be music, dancing and a procession to the temple. No-one will work. Beautiful animals, washed and draped with garlands of flowers, wine, oil, honey and barley cakes will be burnt as sacrifices on altars in the open air. The priests may let you eat the left-overs – a real feast.

Artemis was Apollo's sister. A fierce huntress, she protected wild animals and girls.

Ares was the god of war. He was brave, angry and terrible. He protected soldiers.

Aphrodite was the beautiful goddess of love. She inspired and protected lovers everywhere.

Demeter was an ancient corn-goddess. She protected the crops in the fields.

Hermes was the swift, silent messenger of the gods; he reported events on earth.

Poseidon was god of earthquakes and the sea. Protector of sailors, he sent shipwrecks too.

GODS AND GODDESSES
WHAT WOULD YOU BELIEVE IN?

A S AN ANCIENT GREEK, you said prayers at your family's altars, offered sacrifices at temples, took part in public festivals, and visited oracles at ancient holy sites. You expected religion to be useful. You hoped your prayers or vigils would make your life better now and not in heaven after your death.

In a magical way, taking part in ceremonies gave you power. If you made the right offerings, you obliged the gods, or the mysterious spirits who lived at holy places, to help you in return.

As an ancient Greek, you might believe that oracles foretold the future. The most famous oracle, a woman (the Pythia) drugged by smoke from burning laurel leaves, spoke for the god Apollo. Priests interpreted her words. People came to consult her at the great temple of Delphi (below).

AT THE TEMPLE of Zeus at Dodona, the god spoke by rustling the leaves of sacred oak trees. Write your questions on a slab of lead; the priests will listen to the trees, then answer 'Yes' or 'No'.

NOT ALL FESTIVALS were celebrated with cheerful processions. If you wanted to ask a favour from some gods, you had to face a mysterious, terrifying, ritual.

Your beliefs were also part of your social identity. There were prayers and festivals – and guardian gods and goddesses – for women, children, warriors and even for city-states. All important events in life, from getting married to bringing in the harvest to winning a war, were marked by religious rites.

The god Dionysius brought wine and drunkenness. His gifts were a blessing and a curse.

Asclepius was the god of medicine. His priests worked as doctors in special healing sanctuaries.

Goat-legged Pan was the god of wild, empty places. The fear you felt there was called 'panic'.

The Muses were nine graceful young women who lived with all the other gods on Mount Parnassus, in northern Greece. They protected arts and crafts – from painting pictures to writing history.

The Fates ruled everyone's destiny. They spun out your life like a thread – then cut it short.

BUILDING TECHNIQUES

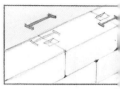

Architects' and builders' tools: dividers, set-square, plumb-line and saw.

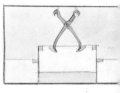

Blocks of stone were joined by strong iron 'ties'. Over the centuries these have rusted, swollen, and split the stone.

Lumps of marble could be lifted using 'claws', which fitted into specially-cut grooves.

Greek builders used a multiple block of pulleys and ropes when lifting carved stones to the top of a tall building.

Q

Why did artists and craftsmen have to know ancient myths and legends about the gods?
Go to pages 22-23

GODS AND GODDESSES 35

If you were ill, you might go to the temple at Epidaurus, and hope to see a vision of the god Asclepius.

You might hear the famous story told by priests about a man whose hand was touched and cured by the god in a dream.

Or they might tell you about the woman whose eye was healed by the god; he told her to give him a silver pig in thanks.

One little boy was cured only after promising to return in one year's time to offer to the god anything he asked.

Q

Would you prefer to go to school or stay at home and learn how to help on the farm?
Go to pages 14-15

(Above) Doctor examining a patient. Greek doctors studied a wide range of medical sciences – anatomy, physiology, surgery, pathology and epidemiology – during their training.
(Below) Medical instruments, including spatulas, probes and a pestle and mortar.

Patients who had been cured by their overnight stay at a temple hospital gave thank-offerings, called 'ex-votos', in the shape of the body parts which had been healed. Often they threw money into the temple's holy fountain, too.

SCIENCE AND MEDICINE
WHO MIGHT YOU LEARN WITH?

IN THE 6TH CENTURY BC, scholars and philosophers began to ask challenging questions, like 'What was the origin of life?' or 'If horses could draw, how would they portray their gods?'. At the same time, scientists were making great discoveries about 'natural laws' in mathematics, music and medicine. These laws showed clearly and logically how the world worked – and they had nothing to do with the unpredictable magic of religion. A new, scientific, way of looking at the world was developing. Students travelled vast distances to learn from the great thinkers at 'academies' and colleges. But many scientists and philosophers were regarded as dangerous revolutionaries by citizens and their rulers.

Some doctors were more scientific. They tried to work out why illnesses happened at certain times of year.

They believed that the weather, especially warm or cold winds, could affect people's health.

They knew that water from some streams was very pure, but that others were polluted and unhealthy.

They believed that the soil where you lived might make you ill. This could be true, if it lacked vital minerals.

Too much sun, or a life spent shut indoors, might also be bad for you. Greeks encouraged a healthy balance.

Some people today think that attitude affects your health. The Greeks first said this over 2,500 years ago.

GREEK MATHEMATICS

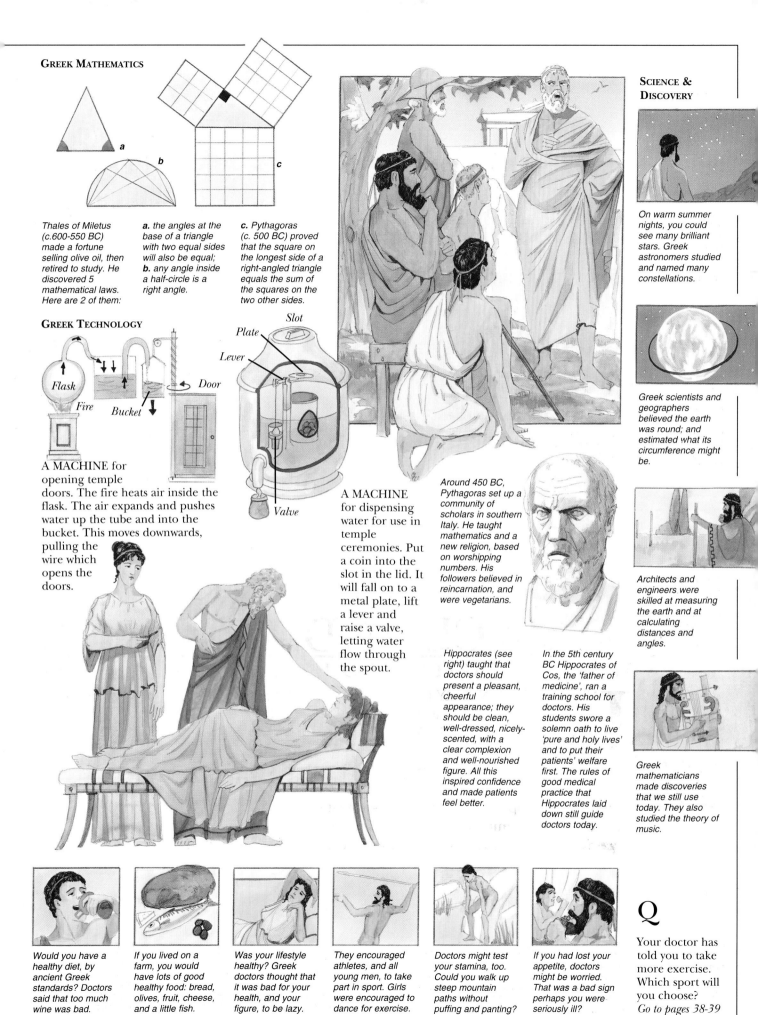

Thales of Miletus (c.600-550 BC) made a fortune selling olive oil, then retired to study. He discovered 5 mathematical laws. Here are 2 of them:

***a.** the angles at the base of a triangle with two equal sides will also be equal;*
***b.** any angle inside a half-circle is a right angle.*

***c.** Pythagoras (c. 500 BC) proved that the square on the longest side of a right-angled triangle equals the sum of the squares on the two other sides.*

GREEK TECHNOLOGY

Flask
Fire
Bucket
Door

A MACHINE for opening temple doors. The fire heats air inside the flask. The air expands and pushes water up the tube and into the bucket. This moves downwards, pulling the wire which opens the doors.

Slot
Plate
Lever
Valve

A MACHINE for dispensing water for use in temple ceremonies. Put a coin into the slot in the lid. It will fall on to a metal plate, lift a lever and raise a valve, letting water flow through the spout.

Around 450 BC, Pythagoras set up a community of scholars in southern Italy. He taught mathematics and a new religion, based on worshipping numbers. His followers believed in reincarnation, and were vegetarians.

Hippocrates (see right) taught that doctors should present a pleasant, cheerful appearance; they should be clean, well-dressed, nicely-scented, with a clear complexion and well-nourished figure. All this inspired confidence and made patients feel better.

In the 5th century BC Hippocrates of Cos, the 'father of medicine', ran a training school for doctors. His students swore a solemn oath to live 'pure and holy lives' and to put their patients' welfare first. The rules of good medical practice that Hippocrates laid down still guide doctors today.

On warm summer nights, you could see many brilliant stars. Greek astronomers studied and named many constellations.

Greek scientists and geographers believed the earth was round; and estimated what its circumference might be.

Architects and engineers were skilled at measuring the earth and at calculating distances and angles.

Greek mathematicians made discoveries that we still use today. They also studied the theory of music.

Would you have a healthy diet, by ancient Greek standards? Doctors said that too much wine was bad.

If you lived on a farm, you would have lots of good healthy food: bread, olives, fruit, cheese, and a little fish.

Was your lifestyle healthy? Greek doctors thought that it was bad for your health, and your figure, to be lazy.

They encouraged athletes, and all young men, to take part in sport. Girls were encouraged to dance for exercise.

Doctors might test your stamina, too. Could you walk up steep mountain paths without puffing and panting?

If you had lost your appetite, doctors might be worried. That was a bad sign perhaps you were seriously ill?

Q

Your doctor has told you to take more exercise. Which sport will you choose?
Go to pages 38-39

What would your favourite sport be? Do you have a strong back and arms? Could you throw a discus?

Or can you run fast and aim straight? Have you practised throwing spears for war? Maybe you'd prefer the javelin?

How good do you think you would be at lifting heavy weights?

Or what about the long-jump? You need to be very fit to do well in that competition.

Q

You live overseas. How would you travel to the Olympic Games?

Go to pages 28-29

SPORTS AND GAMES
WOULD YOU LIKE TO TAKE PART?

AS A GREEK MAN, you would think sport very important. So important, that wars were halted to let the greatest sports festival, the Olympic Games, take place. Other games, held at Corinth and Delphi, were good, manly training for fitness and for fighting. Games were also a chance to show off your skills, or, if you just came to watch, an excuse for an exciting holiday trip. Foreigners were not allowed to attend the Olympics, though overseas Greek colonists travelled long distances to take part. All competitors trained hard, and hoped to win; then as now, becoming a sports hero was one way in which a poor, unknown man could become rich and famous. The most prestigious event was the 200-metre sprint. Cheating and trying to bribe a referee were major crimes for which you would be banished from the Games. But we know, from the remains of statues paid for by the fines of convicted cheats, that sometimes foul play did happen.

Maybe you prefer to sit and watch? The Greeks liked to watch fighting quail. Today, we might say that was cruel.

Or would you choose a team game? Groups of young men played a fast and furious sport rather like hockey.

Another favourite Greek team game was played on piggy-back with a ball. Two teams fought for the ball,

which was thrown into play by an older man. This reconstruction is from a vase-painting.

Boys and girls played knuckle bones (like modern fivestones or jacks). They used small (cleaned)

bones from sheep. Adults played the game, too, and bet on how the bones would fall, and who would win.

IF YOU WON a race at the Olympics, your name would be shouted out by an announcer (usually an important man himself – such as an old war hero). He would also announce the name of your family and the city you came from, so that everyone connected with you could share your glory. You would be given a 'crown' of ribbons and leaves to wear, and rich prizes – oil, pottery, fine fabrics – at the end of the Games.

AT THE OLYMPICS

Wrestling was popular at village festivals, as well as at the Olympics. Greek-style, it was rough and dangerous.

Would you like to fight a Greek boxer? He did not wear gloves, but padded his hands with strips of cloth.

After the excitement of the big race or the big fight, perhaps a peaceful game of draughts would be restful?

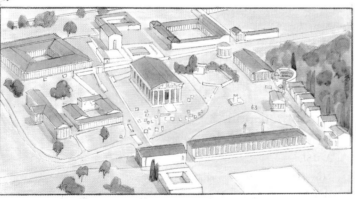

THE VAST COMPLEX at Olympia contained Zeus's temple, rooms for visitors, a camp site, space for market stalls, sports tracks, and a stadium for male spectators to watch events. Women could not attend.

(Left) Victors' crowns were made of laurel leaves, and were sacred to the gods.

Famous athletes were in demand as artists' models; the Greeks admired beautiful bodies.

Or you could join the crowd betting on a cock-fight. This is another ancient Greek sport we would consider cruel today.

If you wanted to take part in the Olympic Games, you had to obey strict rules. First, no fighting.

Next, because the Games are in honour of the gods, you had to promise to respect the temple sanctuary.

Q

You could not take any weapons to the Games. This stopped competitors from rival cities fighting each other.

The Olympic priests declared that the gods would curse any competitor or spectator who broke these rules.

If you did get into a fight, accidentally or on purpose, you would have to pay a heavy fine to the temple.

You should also respect the 'Olympic Peace' protecting travellers to the Games. They must not be attacked.

Q

You're good at throwing the javelin, so you decide to join the army. Is a hoplite's life hard?
Go to pages 32-33

Red-figure vase from Athens, made in the 4th century BC. It shows a woman (left) and a satyr (right) on either side of an altar, making a sacrifice of food to the gods. There is a wineskin hanging from a tree, and a column, topped by a statue, in the background. Vase-paintings like these give us many details of ancient Greek life.

Coins are always useful sources of information.

Each city-state minted its own, with its own symbol. This can show patterns of trade, if, for example, numbers of Athenian coins are found in ports or market-places of other city-states.

One of the most famous Greek statues ever made was this spear-carrier, cast in bronze by the sculptor Polyclitus around 440 BC. It shows his idea of the perfect man: graceful, well-proportioned and athletic. The original statue has been lost; all that survives is a copy, made about 500 years after Polyclitus lived, by Roman artists who admired it.

Greek writing on papyrus has generally not survived because papyrus rots in damp conditions. But a few fragments have been preserved. (Above) This is one of the oldest-known examples, written around 350 BC.

But we do have many other, longer-lasting, examples of Greek writing: a wide range of inscriptions carved on stone.

HOW DO WE KNOW?

THE 'GOLDEN AGE' OF ATHENS was over by 400 BC. Greece was conquered by neighbouring Macedon in 338 BC. Greece was no longer rich and powerful, it was not even independent. Yet this was not 'the end'. In some ways, ancient Greek civilisation is still alive today, almost 2,500 years later. Greek philosophy, mathematics, science, political ideas, and artistic and architectural styles are all still influential.

How has this happened? Partly because Greek philosophers and historians wrote books discussing their own times, which are still read today. We can also use other Greek writings, poems and plays, to find out about Greek peoples' attitudes to their own society. Many beautiful objects, from massive temples and theatres to tiny, delicate coins and jewels have survived.

But there is another reason. Greek culture has been 'adopted' by other, later civilisations, and has become part of them. We still use Greek words today, from 'mega' (very big) to 'micro' (very small). Many buildings designed to impress – banks, colleges, stately homes and even churches – have been made to look like ancient Greek temples. For centuries, people have been taught that if something is inspired by ancient Greece, it must be excellent.

Cargoes from ships wrecked in ancient Greek times have been preserved deep under water beneath layers of sand.

Arms and armour have been found at sites on the Greek mainland and at colonies overseas: **a.** helmet from Corinth; **b.** helmet from Olympia; **c.** sword from Italy; **d.** spear-tip from Italy.

Greek potters made many realistic terracotta (baked clay) figures showing scenes from everyday life. This little statue shows a mother giving good advice to her daughter. We can learn a lot about Greek clothes and hairstyles from objects like this.

Mosaic panels, used to decorate the floors and walls of fine buildings, often provide detailed information which we can use to help us find out more accurately about Greek objects – like ships, houses and great temples – which have only survived in a damaged or ruined condition.

(Right) Carving from the Parthenon temple in Athens (pictured below). Visiting ancient sites lets us admire Greek craft-workers' skills. It also reveals how Greek artists and architects used their art to comment on their own recent history. This carving shows a fight between civilised people and centaurs (monsters). It was made when Athens was celebrating a 'victory' over 'barbarian' invaders.

The Parthenon, Athens

HAVE YOU SURVIVED?

Q1 A hoplite is:

A a good dancer?
B an athlete who takes part in the high-jump?
C a soldier?

Q2 You want to make music. Would you catch:

A a bird?
B a tortoise?
C a sheep?

Q3 You use sea urchins to:

A eat?
B dye cloth purple?
C decorate pottery?

Q4 What is olive oil *not* used for:

A heating houses?
B cooking food?
C cleaning the skin?

Q5 If someone said they wanted to carve a statue of you with no clothes on, would you feel:

A shocked?
B embarrassed?
C flattered?

Q6 Are they making a collar of flowers for that cow to wear:

A because she is a pet?
B because she will soon be sacrificed?
C because they hope it will make her fetch a better price at market?

Q7 Do Spartan mothers tell their sons to die in battle:

A because Spartans don't care whether their sons live or die?
B because Spartans don't know how to nurse battle injuries?
C because Spartans believe death is better than defeat?

Q8 The first Marathon race was named after:

A a famous athlete?
B the site of an important battle?
C the prize of sweet food given to the winner?

Q9 The Athenian assembly was:

A a place where political decisions were made?
B a religious festival?
C a meeting place for families?

Q10 My sister has been out without a sunshade. Our parents are very cross. Is this because:

A she will get sunstroke?
B she will look like a peasant?
C she will spoil her nice new peplos?

To find out if you have survived as an ancient Greek check the answers on page 48.

All dates are BC

c.800-700 Poet known as 'Homer' collects together and writes down fragments of older poems (traditionally passed on by word of mouth), the *Iliad* and the *Odyssey*, telling of heroes and their adventures.

c.800-700 Rise of the Greek city-state.

776 Traditional date of the first Olympic Games, though they may have been held, unrecorded, for at least 500 years before this date.

c.700 New way of fighting introduced, using a 'wall' (called a phalanx) of ordinary citizen foot soldiers (hoplites) instead of noblemen on horseback.

c.700-600 Hesiod, a famous poet, writes poem *Works and Days*, giving advice for a life of honest work.

c.600-500 The hoplites support new rulers, called tyrants, who get rid of old-style kings and nobles.

c.600-500 Philosophers and scientists make major discoveries in mathematics, physics, astronomy and medicine.

c.590 Coins first used in Greece.

c.550-500 Poet Sappho lives and works on island of Lesbos.

c.550-400 Great age of Athenian pottery. Fine pots also made in other city-states.

536 Athlete Milon of Croton wins a record six events at the Olympic Games.

510 Cleisthenes reforms government of Athens as a democracy.

490-449 Greece and Persia at war.

483 Athens builds new fleet.

480-479 Persians invade Greece. They win the battle of Thermopylae, but are crushed by Athenian fleet at sea battle of Salamis, and by Greek hoplites at the land battle of Plataea.

477 Athens heads new alliance against Persia. Athens rapidly takes control, and allied city-states become part of Athens' empire.

462 Politician and war leader Pericles (c.500-429) wins support of the assembly in Athens; becomes leader of the city until his death.

450-400 Golden age of Athenian drama, sculpture and architecture.

447 Building work begins at the Parthenon.

430-423 Plague in Athens; many die.

431 Sparta attacks Athens; start of the First Peloponnesian War (ends 421 BC, though the cities are still bitter rivals).

413 Sparta builds fort on Athenian land; Second Peloponnesian War begins.

404 Second Peloponnesian War ends after Athenian fleet smashed in sea battle by Spartan general, Lysander. Spartan troops surround Athens and starve the citizens into surrender.

350 Kingdom of Macedon (north of Greece) begins to invade neighbouring lands.

338 King Philip of Macedon controls Greece.

336 Alexander, son of Philip of Macedon, inherits kingdom.

GLOSSARY

ABACUS frame with three rows of beads, used as a calculating machine.

ACROPOLIS ('high city') stronghold or fortress built on the highest point in a town. Defended by natural cliffs or strong stone walls. Often (as at Athens) the site of important temples.

ADZE tool with a sharp metal axe-like blade fixed at right-angles to a wooden handle.

ALTAR table or slab of stone, placed outside Greek temples, where sacrifices to the gods were made.

ANCIENT GREEKS people who lived in the land of Greece in the 10th to 3rd centuries BC. This book describes ancient Greek life from around 550 BC – 400 BC.

ARCADE row of arches, usually along one side of a building. Often built to create a shady walkway.

ASIA MINOR the land of present-day Turkey and the islands offshore.

BALLOT small metal or pottery token, about the size of a pebble, used when voting.

BARTER a way of trading: exchanging goods for others of similar value.

BRONZE metal alloy, a mixture of copper and tin.

CAVALRY soldiers who fight on horseback.

CENTAUR mythical monster, half man (the front), half horse (the back).

CHAFF dry, papery outer casing surrounding grains of wheat and barley. Removed by threshing.

CHITON loose, flowing tunic, worn short by men and long by women.

CHORUS team of singers and dancers who played an important part in Greek drama.

CITIZEN adult male who lived in a city-state and had the right to take part in political decision-making at the assembly.

Women, slaves and foreigners did not have these rights.

CITY-STATE a self-governing city and the surrounding land.

COLONY territory ruled by people from another country.

DEMOCRACY government by the people.

DIADEM jewellery or hair ornament worn like a headband.

DOWRY gift given by a bride's father to her new husband or his family.

EPHEBE young man aged between 15 and 20 who might be called up for military service.

EPIDEMIOLOGY the scientific study of mass outbreaks of disease.

EX-VOTO thank-offering (usually in the shape of a body part) hung up in temples and dedicated to the god of healing.

FIBROUS tough, woody and stringy.

GALLEY wide-bodied ship, powered by oars and sails.

GORGON mythical monster, with a woman's face surrounded by 'hair' of poisonous snakes.

GREAVES armour to protect the lower legs.

HETAIRIAI educated, elegant, unmarried women, mistresses and (sometimes) advisors to wealthy or powerful men.

HIMATION long cloak.

HOPLITE soldier who fought on foot.

KITHARA musical instrument with strings.

KOTTABOS game (throwing wine at a target) played at symposia (dinner parties).

LOTTERY way of choosing (or awarding prizes) by chance.

LYRE musical instrument made from a tortoise shell.

MOSAIC picture or pattern made from thousands of tiny fragments of coloured glass, clay tiles or pebbles.

MULE animal used to carry heavy loads, bred from a donkey mated with a horse.

OLIGARCHY government by a small group of influential people.

ORACLE place where ancient Greeks could find out what lay in the future. People consulting an oracle hoped to receive a message or sign from the gods.

OSTRACISE to punish by sending someone away from their homeland for ten years.

PANNIER large basket carried on the sides of donkeys or mules.

PAPYRUS paper made from reeds.

PATHOLOGY the study of disease and how it damages the human body.

PELTAST soldier who fought with a spear or by hurling stones from a sling.

PEPLOS long overtunic worn by women.

PHYSIOLOGY the study of how the human body works.

PORTICO covered porch.

QUAIL small migratory bird, trapped in nets, cooked and eaten.

REINCARNATION being born again after death, but in a different body.

SACRIFICE offering, usually an animal or special food, given to the gods in the hope of winning their favour or averting their anger.

SANCTUARY the holiest part of a temple or other holy site.

SATYR mythical creature, a goat-like man, with big ears and a long tail. Rude and boisterous.

SHRINE holy site, where a god or goddess is worshipped.

SYMPOSIUM (plural SYMPOSIA) A dinner party for men. Sometimes for serious discussions, other times for drunken entertainment.

TRIDENT weapon like a spear with three sharp prongs.

TRIREME warship powered by men rowing three banks of oars.

VIGIL staying awake all night, usually as part of a religious ritual.

INDEX

ANSWERS
HAVE YOU SURVIVED?

Here are the quiz answers, with pages to turn to if you need an explanation.

1 (C) – pages 32-33.
2 (B) – pages 40-41.
3 (B) – pages 26-27.
4 (A) – pages 14-15.
5 (C if male, A if female) – pages 20-21.
6 (B) – pages 34-35.
7 (C) – pages 18-19.
8 (B) – pages 32-33.
9 (A) – pages 30-31.
10 (B) – pages 20-21.

Count up your correct answers and find out what your survival rating is.

9 - 10   You will make an excellent ancient Greek.
6 - 8   You will be a capable member of society.
3 - 5   Keep your head down and try to stay out of trouble.
0 - 2   Likely to be ostracised.

ACKNOWLEDGEMENTS

The Salariya Book Co Ltd would like to thank Sarah Ridley for her assistance.